The Quantum Financial Revolution

Unlocking the Power of the Future

I0409838

By Ben Davis

Contents

Chapter 1: The Quantum Financial Landscape

An introduction to the current state of finance and the potential for quantum computing to revolutionize the industry.

In the vast landscape of finance, traditional computing has played a pivotal role in powering the financial world as we know it today. However, as we stand on the cusp of a new era, quantum computing emerges as a disruptive force, offering unimaginable possibilities for the future. The intersection of quantum physics and finance promises to unlock a realm of untapped potential, reshaping the way we think about money, investments, and the very fabric of the financial industry.

The current state of finance is built upon the foundation of classical computing, where information is processed through binary digits, or bits, which represent either a 0 or a 1. These bits, combined in complex algorithms, allow us to execute financial transactions, analyze markets, and manage risk. Yet, despite the tremendous power of classical computing, it struggles to tackle certain intricacies of financial problems efficiently.

Enter quantum computing, which harnesses the fundamental principles of quantum mechanics to process information in a radically different way. Instead of binary bits, quantum bits, or qubits, can exist in a superposition of 0 and 1 simultaneously, offering a multitude of potential states. Moreover, qubits can become entangled, enabling them to share information instantaneously, even across vast distances. These quantum phenomena have the potential to redefine the landscape of finance, transforming the traditional tools and strategies we have relied upon for decades.

One area where quantum computing shows great promise is in the field of optimization, a crucial component of finance. Many financial decisions involve finding optimal solutions within vast sets of variables and constraints. Classical computers struggle to handle these complex optimization problems, often resorting to approximate solutions with limited accuracy. Quantum computers, on the other hand, can efficiently explore the vast solution space, seeking the optimal answer with remarkable speed and precision.

Imagine a world where investment portfolios can be optimized in real-time, factoring in a myriad of variables such as market fluctuations, risk profiles, and investor preferences. Quantum computing could revolutionize portfolio management, enabling investors to make informed decisions quickly and with unprecedented accuracy. Equally transformative is the potential for quantum machine learning algorithms, which could uncover hidden patterns and correlations within financial data, empowering analysts and traders with unparalleled insights.

However, the realization of the quantum financial revolution is not without its challenges. Quantum computers are delicate systems that require carefully controlled environments, extreme cold temperatures, and intricate error correction mechanisms. Overcoming these technical hurdles, along with ensuring the security of quantum networks, are crucial steps to fully harnessing the potential of quantum computing within the financial industry.

As we delve deeper into the realms of this quantum financial landscape, we are poised at the precipice of a paradigm shift. Beyond optimization and machine learning, quantum computing could also disrupt cryptography, risk assessment, fraud detection, and derivative pricing, among other areas. The potential impact extends far beyond finance, with implications for supply chain management, drug discovery, and climate modeling, to name just a few.

The quantum financial landscape presents a vast expanse of uncharted territory. In the second half of this chapter, we will explore the cutting-edge developments in quantum computing, the challenges we face, and the transformative potential that lies ahead. Prepare to dive into a world where the unimaginable becomes within reach, where the power of quantum mechanics converges with finance, forever changing the way we interact with money, investments, and the very essence of our economic systems.As we continue our journey through the quantum financial landscape, we begin to grasp the potential of this groundbreaking technology. In this second half of the chapter, we will delve deeper into the cutting-edge developments in quantum computing, explore the challenges we face, and further examine the transformative potential that lies ahead.

One of the key challenges in realizing the quantum financial revolution is the development of practical and scalable quantum computers. Currently, quantum computers are limited in terms of their qubit count and error rates. However, significant progress is being made by both academic researchers and industry leaders in building larger and more stable systems. As the technology advances, we can expect more powerful quantum computers that can handle increasingly complex financial problems.

Noise, or errors, introduced during the computation process is another obstacle that needs to be overcome. To mitigate these errors, quantum error correction techniques are being developed to ensure the accuracy and reliability of quantum computations. These techniques involve encoding information redundantly and implementing error-detection protocols, allowing for the correction of errors as they occur. By addressing these challenges, we can pave the way for a robust and error-resistant quantum computing infrastructure.

Security is a paramount concern in the realm of finance, and the quantum financial revolution is no exception. Quantum computers possess the potential to break current encryption methods, rendering traditional cryptographic systems vulnerable. However, researchers are actively working on developing quantum-resistant cryptographic algorithms, known as post-quantum cryptography, to protect sensitive financial data from quantum attacks. These new algorithms utilize mathematical problems that are believed to be difficult for both classical and quantum computers to solve, ensuring the security of our financial transactions in a quantum-powered world.

Furthermore, collaborations between academia, industry, and government bodies are crucial to navigating the challenges of the quantum financial landscape. Initiatives such as quantum research centers and incubators are instrumental in fostering innovation, knowledge sharing, and technological advancements. By fostering these collaborations, we can accelerate the development and implementation of quantum solutions in the financial industry.

The transformative potential of quantum computing within the financial sector reaches far beyond optimization and machine learning. Risk assessment stands to benefit significantly from quantum capabilities, enabling more accurate predictions and better-informed investment decisions. Fraud detection systems could also leverage quantum algorithms to identify suspicious patterns in real-time, enhancing the security of our financial systems and protecting against malicious activities.

Derivative pricing, a complex and integral aspect of finance, can also be revolutionized by quantum computing. Traditional pricing models often rely on simplified assumptions and approximations, leading to limitations in accuracy. Quantum algorithms, with their ability to explore vast solution spaces efficiently, can provide more precise and accurate valuations, reducing uncertainty and improving market efficiency.

Beyond finance, the impact of quantum computing holds vast implications for various industries. Supply chain management could benefit from improved optimization algorithms, leading to more efficient logistics and reduced costs. In drug discovery, quantum simulations can unravel complex molecular interactions, accelerating the development of new medications. Climate modeling can harness the power of quantum computers to simulate and predict climate patterns with greater accuracy, aiding in the fight against climate change.

As we conclude this chapter on the quantum financial landscape, we stand in awe of the immense potential that lies ahead. The fusion of quantum mechanics and finance presents us with an unprecedented opportunity to redefine the way we interact with money, investments, and the very foundation of our economic systems. While challenges remain, it is the collaborative efforts of brilliant minds, industry leaders, and policymakers that will propel us further into this uncharted territory.

Embrace this brave new world, where the power of quantum computing holds the key to unlocking untold possibilities. Join us as we embark on a thrilling journey towards a quantum financial revolution, destined to shape the future of finance and transform the way we navigate the intricate realm of money, investments, and the global economy.

Together, let us harness the power of quantum mechanics and embark on a path of endless discovery and innovation. The quantum financial revolution beckons, and it is time for us to embrace the future that awaits.

Chapter 2: Understanding Quantum Computing

Technology is constantly evolving, and with each passing day, new innovations push the boundaries of what we previously deemed impossible. One such groundbreaking advancement is quantum computing – a phenomenon poised to revolutionize our world and unlock the power of the future. In this chapter, we will delve into the fundamental concepts and principles behind quantum computing, providing a basic understanding for readers who are eager to explore this fascinating realm.

To comprehend quantum computing, it is essential to grasp the principles of quantum mechanics, a branch of physics that describes the behavior of matter and energy at the smallest scales. Unlike classical computers that rely on traditional bits (0s and 1s), quantum computers store and process information using quantum bits, also known as qubits. While a classical bit can exist in either a 0 or 1 state, a qubit can be in a superposition of both states simultaneously. This unique characteristic allows quantum computers to perform complex calculations at an exponential speed compared to their classical counterparts.

The power of quantum computing emanates from the phenomenon called quantum entanglement. Entanglement occurs when two or more qubits become linked, regardless of the distance between them. This interconnectedness enables quantum computers to solve intricate problems by exploiting the correlations between these entangled qubits. It is as if the qubits share an invisible bond that allows them to communicate and influence each other instantaneously.

Another crucial concept in quantum computing is quantum superposition. As mentioned earlier, qubits can exist in multiple states simultaneously. This ability to exist in a superposition of states enables quantum computers to perform parallel computations. While a classical computer solves problems sequentially, executing one step at a time, quantum computers can explore countless possibilities simultaneously using superposition. This parallelism boosts their computational capacity exponentially.

While quantum computing holds immense potential, it also faces significant challenges. One notable issue is quantum decoherence, which occurs when a qubit loses its delicate quantum state and collapses into a classical state due to environmental interference. To mitigate the effects of decoherence, researchers are actively exploring various approaches like error correction codes and fault-tolerant systems, which aim to preserve and protect the fragile quantum information.

Scientists and researchers around the globe are working tirelessly to harness the power of quantum computing. Its applications span a wide array of fields, including cryptography, optimization, drug discovery, and climate modeling. With the anticipated advent of practical quantum computers, we may witness breakthroughs in areas previously thought to be insurmountable.

So long as we strive to understand the underpinnings of quantum computing, we embark on a journey towards a future that is limitless in its potential. Stay tuned as we continue to explore the exciting realm of quantum computing, unraveling its intricacies and uncovering its fascinating implications. In the second half of this chapter, we will delve into the practical applications and ongoing research propelling us further into the quantum era.

Remember, this is not the end of the chapter; it is merely the beginning of a remarkable voyage of discovery. Together, let us unlock the power of the future and embrace the quantum financial revolution that lies ahead.With a foundational understanding of the principles and concepts behind quantum computing, let us embark on a deeper exploration of its practical applications and ongoing research. The potential of quantum computing to revolutionize various fields is both thrilling and astounding.

One area that stands to benefit greatly from quantum computing is cryptography. Traditional cryptographic methods rely on complex algorithms that are difficult for classical computers to break. However, as the power of classical computers continues to increase, these algorithms may eventually become vulnerable. Quantum computers, on the other hand, have the potential to solve mathematical problems at an exponentially faster rate, threatening the security of current cryptographic systems.

Quantum cryptography, which leverages the principles of quantum mechanics, offers a promising solution. By using qubits to transmit secure cryptographic keys, quantum communication protocols can ensure the unconditional security of data transmission. This advancement holds immense potential for secure communication and could transform the way we protect sensitive information in the digital age.

In addition to cryptography, quantum computing also holds promise in the field of optimization. Many real-world problems involve finding the most efficient solution among countless possibilities. Classical computers struggle with these complex optimization challenges, often settling for approximations. Quantum computers, with their parallel processing capabilities and ability to explore multiple solutions simultaneously, could provide optimal solutions more efficiently.

Industries such as logistics, finance, and transportation could significantly benefit from quantum optimization. For instance, routing algorithms that minimize travel time or energy consumption could have a profound impact on the efficiency of delivery services and transportation networks. Portfolio optimization in finance could also be revolutionized, enabling investors to make better-informed decisions and potentially maximizing returns.

Another area where quantum computing is making significant strides is drug discovery. Developing new pharmaceuticals is an expensive and time-consuming process, relying heavily on computational simulations and analysis. Quantum computing can enhance the accuracy and efficiency of these simulations, leading to the discovery of novel drug candidates and potentially accelerating the development of life-saving treatments.

By simulating the behavior of molecules with high precision, quantum computers can provide valuable insights into their interactions, structures, and properties. This knowledge can aid in the design of more effective drugs, enhance personalized medicine, and contribute to the fight against diseases that have defied previous treatment approaches.

Furthermore, quantum computing has the potential to revolutionize climate modeling, aiding our understanding of complex weather patterns and climate change. Climate models involve vast amounts of data and computations, posing significant challenges for classical computers. Quantum computers' vast computational power and the ability to handle large datasets simultaneously can accelerate climate simulations, improve prediction accuracy, and inform policies to mitigate the effects of climate change.

As researchers and scientists continue to push the boundaries of quantum computing, the future holds countless possibilities. However, it is important to acknowledge that we are still at the early stages of harnessing the true potential of this revolutionary technology. Many challenges lie ahead, including addressing the practical limitations of current quantum systems, developing error correction methods, and improving qubit stability.

Nevertheless, the ongoing research and progress in the field of quantum computing inspire optimism. With collaborations across academia, industry, and government, we are steadily paving the way towards the realization of practical quantum computers that can unlock unprecedented computational power.

In conclusion, quantum computing not only captivates the imagination but also holds significant promise in various sectors. From cryptography to optimization, drug discovery to climate modeling, the potential applications are vast and transformative. As we delve further into the quantum era, an era driven by superposition, entanglement, and quantum mechanics, let us remain steadfast in our pursuit of knowledge and embrace the limitless possibilities that lie ahead. Together, we can unlock the power of the future and propel ourselves into the quantum financial revolution.

Chapter 3: The Role of Quantum Computing in Finance

In the ever-evolving landscape of finance, quantum computing emerges as a groundbreaking technology that has the potential to revolutionize the industry. With its extraordinary processing power and ability to analyze vast amounts of data, quantum computing holds the key to unlocking new frontiers in portfolio optimization, risk management, and fraud detection.

Portfolio optimization, a fundamental aspect of finance, aims to maximize investment returns while minimizing risk. Traditional methods often fall short due to their limited capacity to handle complex calculations and navigate the intricacies of market dynamics. However, with the integration of quantum computing, this paradigm is set to change. By harnessing the principles of quantum mechanics, scientists and researchers have developed algorithms that can efficiently optimize portfolios, considering numerous factors such as asset volatility, correlation, and liquidity. This cutting-edge approach empowers investors to make more informed decisions, ultimately leading to enhanced returns and reduced exposure to risk.

Risk management, another critical component of the financial world, heavily relies on accurate predictions, scenario analysis, and stress testing. Quantum computing offers a significant advantage in this field by enabling analysts to perform complex simulations and computations, enabling them to identify potential risks and mitigate them proactively. With its unparalleled computational capabilities, quantum computers can swiftly analyze vast datasets, factor in multiple variables, and generate comprehensive risk assessment models. By providing more accurate and precise forecasts, quantum computing empowers financial institutions to make informed risk management strategies and safeguard their assets effectively.

Fraud detection, a constant battle for financial institutions, can also benefit immensely from the power of quantum computing. The rise of digital transactions and sophisticated fraudulent activities pose significant challenges to conventional detection methods. Quantum computing introduces a new dimension of analysis, enabling financial organizations to identify intricate patterns and anomalies that typically go unnoticed. By leveraging quantum algorithms, institutions can process vast quantities of transactional data, scan for irregularities, and flag potential fraudulent activities more efficiently. This allows for early intervention, preventing financial losses and safeguarding the integrity of the system.

As quantum computing continues to advance, its potential applications in finance are far-reaching. The enhanced computational capacity and advanced algorithmic capabilities offered by quantum computers have the power to transform traditional finance practices. With the ability to solve complex problems at an accelerated pace, quantum computing can facilitate faster and more accurate decision-making, leading to improved financial outcomes.

However, despite its immense potential, quantum computing in finance is not without challenges. Quantum systems are notoriously delicate, susceptible to errors caused by external disturbances. Overcoming these technical obstacles and optimizing the performance of quantum computers remains a persistent area of research and development.

In the second half of this chapter, we will delve deeper into the practical implementation of quantum computing in finance, exploring real-world examples and the implications it holds for the industry. Join us as we unravel the mysteries of this transformative technology and uncover how it promises to reshape the financial landscape as we know it. Stay tuned for the exciting exploration that awaits in the second part of this chapter.As we delve deeper into the practical implementation of quantum computing in finance, the transformative potential of this technology becomes even more apparent. Real-world examples highlight the implications that quantum computing holds for the financial industry, showcasing its ability to revolutionize traditional practices and drive unprecedented advancements.

One area where quantum computing is poised to make a significant impact is in the realm of algorithmic trading. Algorithmic trading involves the use of complex mathematical models to automate trading processes and make investment decisions. With the integration of quantum computing, these models can be greatly improved, enabling traders to analyze vast amounts of historical market data, spot hidden patterns, and make more accurate predictions. By harnessing the superior computational power of quantum computers, algorithmic trading strategies can be fine-tuned to achieve higher returns and mitigate risks associated with market volatility.

In addition to algorithmic trading, quantum computing presents exciting opportunities in the field of computational finance. Financial institutions heavily rely on complex computational models to price derivatives, assess risk exposure, and determine optimal investment strategies. Quantum computers offer the ability to solve complex mathematical equations quickly and accurately, providing more efficient pricing models and risk management frameworks. This enables financial institutions to navigate rapidly changing market conditions with greater agility and precision.

Another promising application of quantum computing in finance lies in the field of cryptography. As digital transactions become increasingly prevalent, ensuring the security and privacy of sensitive financial information is of paramount importance. Quantum computers have the potential to dramatically impact the field of cryptography by breaking traditional encryption algorithms, making current security measures obsolete. However, quantum researchers and cryptographers are also working on developing quantum-resistant cryptographic algorithms to counter this future threat, ensuring the continued security of digital financial transactions.

Furthermore, quantum computing can contribute significantly to the optimization of financial operations and resource allocation. With its unparalleled computing power, it can efficiently solve optimization problems related to resource allocation, supply chain management, and logistics. By analyzing vast amounts of data and factoring in various constraints, quantum computers can provide financial institutions with optimized solutions that minimize costs, maximize efficiency, and streamline processes.

As we explore the practical implementation of quantum computing in finance, it is important to acknowledge the challenges and limitations that accompany this technology. One of the most significant obstacles is the development of error-correcting codes and fault-tolerant quantum systems. Quantum computers are notoriously susceptible to errors caused by external disturbances and decoherence, which can hinder their computational accuracy. Overcoming these technical barriers remains an area of ongoing research and development, striving to optimize the performance and reliability of quantum computing systems.

In conclusion, quantum computing presents a transformative opportunity for the financial industry. From portfolio optimization and risk management to fraud detection and algorithmic trading, the applications of quantum computing hold the promise of enhanced decision-making, improved financial outcomes, and strengthened security measures. As the field of quantum computing continues to evolve, it is crucial for financial institutions to stay aware of its developments and embrace this technology to unlock its tremendous potential. And with that, we conclude our exploration of quantum computing in finance, leaving you with a glimpse into the remarkable possibilities that lie ahead.

Chapter 4: Unleashing the Power of Quantum Algorithms

The world of finance is on the precipice of a revolution, one that is set to redefine the way we approach complex computations and problem-solving. At the heart of this quantum leap forward lies the untapped potential of quantum algorithms. These revolutionary algorithms are poised to unlock a new era of possibilities, allowing us to solve computational challenges that were previously deemed insurmountable. In this chapter, we delve deep into the fascinating realm of quantum algorithms, exploring two key algorithms that hold tremendous promise for the financial industry: Grover's algorithm and Shor's algorithm.

Let us first uncover the inner workings of Grover's algorithm, which is specifically designed to search through unstructured databases with remarkable efficiency. Traditional algorithms search through data linearly, checking each element one by one until a match is found. However, Grover's algorithm employs a clever approach leveraging the principles of quantum superposition and interference. By representing the search space as a quantum state, it harnesses the power of quantum parallelism, allowing multiple computations to be performed simultaneously. Through a process of successive iterations, Grover's algorithm efficiently zeroes in on the desired solution, significantly reducing search times from exponential to quadratic. The implications for the financial sector are tremendous, as it offers the potential to accelerate complex data analysis, such as portfolio optimization, fraud detection, and risk assessment, to name but a few.

Now, as we shift our focus to Shor's algorithm, we enter the realm of quantum computing's true superpower – its ability to efficiently factorize large numbers. Factoring large numbers forms the backbone of modern encryption protocols, making Shor's algorithm a potential game-changer in the realm of cybersecurity. While traditional computers struggle to factorize large numbers due to their exponential time complexity, Shor's algorithm operates at an astonishing polynomial time complexity on quantum computers. By leveraging the quantum phenomena of superposition and entanglement, Shor's algorithm finds the prime factors of integers exponentially faster than classical counterparts. The ramifications of this breakthrough are immense, as it undermines the security of many encryption schemes upon which our financial systems rely.

Imagine the tremendous impact these quantum algorithms could have on financial computations. By significantly speeding up computation times and solving problems that were seemingly out of reach, quantum algorithms have the potential to revolutionize trading strategies, optimize investment portfolios, detect market patterns, and enhance risk management protocols. The financial industry stands on the brink of a quantum future, where these algorithms can unlock untold opportunities and propel us into a new era of financial innovation.

As we conclude the first half of this chapter, we have only begun to scratch the surface of the incredible potential that quantum algorithms hold for the financial world. In the second half, we will explore additional quantum algorithms, discussing their unique applications and shedding light on how they can reshape financial computations. Brace yourself for revelations that will reshape the way financial institutions operate and harness the power of the quantum realm. The revolution is just beginning. Stay tuned.Now, as we continue our exploration of quantum algorithms in the realm of finance, we encounter two more powerful algorithms that have the potential to redefine and revolutionize computational capabilities: Quantum Fourier Transform and Quantum Approximate Optimization Algorithm.

The Quantum Fourier Transform (QFT) is a fundamental algorithm in quantum computing that plays a key role in various applications. It is particularly significant in solving problems related to signal processing and optimization. QFT takes advantage of the phenomenon of quantum superposition to process a large number of input signals simultaneously. By transforming the input signal into its frequency domain representation, QFT enables efficient analysis and manipulation of complex financial data.

In the financial sector, QFT can be applied to tasks such as noise reduction, signal filtering, and prediction modeling. With its ability to process multiple signals in parallel, QFT can enhance the accuracy and speed of pattern recognition in market data analysis. This algorithm has the potential to uncover hidden market trends, identify trading opportunities, and optimize investment strategies. By harnessing the power of QFT, financial institutions can gain a competitive edge in a fast-paced and data-driven industry.

Moving on to the Quantum Approximate Optimization Algorithm (QAOA), we delve into the realm of optimization problems that are prevalent in financial computations. From portfolio optimization to risk management, numerous financial scenarios involve finding the most efficient solution from a vast search space. Traditional computing methods often struggle to tackle these complex optimization problems due to the exponential nature of their time complexity.

QAOA offers a promising alternative by leveraging the principles of quantum superposition and entanglement. This algorithm combines classical optimization techniques with quantum computation to efficiently search through numerous possibilities and find near-optimal solutions. With QAOA, financial institutions can streamline processes such as portfolio rebalancing, asset allocation, and risk assessment.

The potential impact of QAOA is far-reaching. By reducing the time needed to solve optimization problems, it enables financial institutions to make faster and more accurate decisions. This could lead to improved investment returns, enhanced risk management, and more efficient allocation of resources. QAOA has the capacity to transform the way financial professionals approach complex decision-making processes, empowering them to navigate dynamic markets with greater precision and agility.

As we reach the conclusion of our exploration into quantum algorithms for finance, we can truly grasp the immense possibilities and opportunities that lie ahead. Grovers algorithm, Shors algorithm, Quantum Fourier Transform, and Quantum Approximate Optimization Algorithm are just the beginning of a new era in computational power. These algorithms have the potential to reshape financial computations, enhance data analysis, and bolster the security of the industry.

The quest for unlocking the power of quantum algorithms in finance continues, as researchers and industry professionals explore new avenues and harness the potential of emerging technologies. The quantum revolution in finance is underway, and its impact will be felt at every level of the industry. Embracing these advancements, financial institutions can gain an unparalleled competitive advantage, maximized profitability, and ensure the robustness and security of their operations.

As we conclude this chapter, we invite you to imagine the possibilities that await us in a future fueled by quantum algorithms. The potential for unlocking new dimensions of financial innovation is immeasurable. Brace yourself for a quantum future where the boundaries of computational capabilities are pushed even further, paving the way for unparalleled growth and progress.

Stay tuned for future chapters where we will delve into more quantum algorithms and their applications in the world of finance. The journey has just begun, and the revolution is unstoppable.

Chapter 5: Quantum Machine Learning in Financial Markets

In recent years, the convergence of quantum computing and machine learning has opened up new frontiers in various industries, including finance. Financial markets, driven by the constant need for accurate predictions and optimal strategies, are increasingly exploring the potential benefits of quantum machine learning techniques. This promising fusion of quantum computing and machine learning holds the key to unlocking unprecedented power for analyzing financial data and making predictions that can reshape the future of trading and investment strategies.

Traditional machine learning algorithms have significantly advanced our understanding of financial markets. However, they are limited by their reliance on classical computing, which struggles to efficiently handle complex data and intricate mathematical models. This is where quantum machine learning comes into play – by harnessing the fundamental principles of quantum mechanics, it has the potential to revolutionize our approach to analyzing financial data.

One of the key advantages quantum machine learning brings to financial markets is its ability to process vast amounts of data simultaneously, leveraging the phenomenon of quantum superposition. In traditional machine learning, data is processed sequentially, which can be time-consuming and limit the depth of analysis. In contrast, quantum machine learning algorithms can simultaneously analyze multiple dimensions of financial data, providing a more comprehensive view of market trends, correlations, and anomalies.

Moreover, the concept of quantum entanglement introduces another dimension to the analysis of financial data. Quantum entanglement refers to the inherent connection between quantum particles, even if separated over vast distances. In the context of finance, this means that interconnected financial variables can be modeled collectively rather than individually, enabling more accurate predictions and risk assessments. By capturing subtle interdependencies across various financial metrics, quantum machine learning can enhance our understanding of complex market dynamics and potentially reveal hidden patterns and opportunities.

Quantum machine learning also offers a significant advantage in optimizing investment strategies. Traditional algorithms typically rely on gradient-based optimization methods, which can sometimes get stuck in suboptimal solutions. Quantum machine learning, however, introduces the concept of quantum annealing, which leverages quantum tunneling to explore a wider range of possible solutions and find the most optimal investment strategies. This ability to explore a vast solution space efficiently can potentially lead to optimized portfolios, risk mitigation, and improved returns for investors.

The application of quantum machine learning techniques in financial markets is still relatively nascent, but the possibilities it presents are undoubtedly captivating. As researchers and practitioners continue to explore and refine quantum machine learning algorithms, we are likely to witness a paradigm shift in the way financial data is analyzed, predictions are made, and investment decisions are executed. The fusion of quantum computing and machine learning holds immense potential to empower financial professionals with unprecedented insights and tools, ultimately revolutionizing the way we navigate the world of finance.

Intriguingly, this is only the beginning. As we delve deeper into the realm of quantum machine learning in financial markets, we will uncover even more astonishing applications and gain a deeper understanding of its implications. The second half of this chapter will explore some of the most cutting-edge developments and real-world experiments in this field, which will undoubtedly ignite your imagination and shed light on the transformative role that quantum machine learning is destined to play in the future of finance. The evolution of financial markets is upon us, and the quantum financial revolution is poised to unlock its remarkable power. Stay tuned for the adventurous journey waiting ahead.The second half of the chapter delves into some of the most cutting-edge developments and real-world experiments in the field of quantum machine learning in financial markets. These advancements not only showcase the transformative potential of quantum machine learning but also demonstrate how it can be applied to tackle complex financial challenges.

One exciting area of exploration in quantum machine learning is portfolio optimization. Traditional methods often struggle to efficiently balance risk and return in a portfolio, leading to suboptimal investment strategies. However, quantum machine learning, with its ability to explore a vast solution space efficiently, presents a promising solution. By leveraging quantum annealing, financial professionals can effectively navigate the complex landscape of investment choices and identify the most optimal combination of assets for a portfolio. This not only helps in maximizing returns but also enhances risk mitigation strategies, promoting more robust financial decisions.

In addition to portfolio optimization, quantum machine learning also offers immense potential in extracting insights from high-dimensional financial data. As financial markets generate an ever-increasing amount of information, traditional algorithms often struggle to identify meaningful patterns and correlations. Quantum machine learning, on the other hand, excels at processing vast amounts of data simultaneously, providing a more comprehensive understanding of market dynamics and uncovering hidden relationships.

Quantum machine learning techniques have also shown promise in the realm of algorithmic trading. The ability to process multiple dimensions of data simultaneously enables more accurate predictions of market trends and anomalies, enhancing the effectiveness of algorithmic trading strategies. By leveraging quantum entanglement, financial professionals can model interconnected financial variables collectively rather than individually, offering a more holistic approach to trading and investment decision-making.

Real-world experiments have already begun to validate the potential of quantum machine learning in financial markets. For instance, researchers at a leading financial institution utilized quantum machine learning algorithms to optimize a portfolio of exchange-traded funds (ETFs). The results surpassed those achieved by traditional methods, highlighting the efficacy of quantum machine learning in portfolio management.

Another noteworthy experiment involved the prediction of stock price movements. A team of researchers used quantum machine learning techniques to analyze historical market data and make short-term predictions on stock prices. The results exhibited higher accuracy compared to conventional machine learning algorithms, showcasing the significant potential of quantum machine learning in financial forecasting.

While these experiments showcase the early successes of quantum machine learning in finance, it is essential to acknowledge that the field is still in its early stages. Further research and development are needed to refine and scale these techniques for widespread adoption. Challenges such as noise suppression, error correction, and hardware limitations remain areas of active exploration.

As the second half of this chapter draws to a close, it is clear that the fusion of quantum computing and machine learning holds immense potential for the future of financial markets. The transformative power of quantum machine learning in analyzing financial data, optimizing investment strategies, and improving risk management cannot be overstated. By embracing the possibilities offered by quantum machine learning, financial professionals can unlock unprecedented insights and tools, ultimately reshaping the landscape of finance.

The quantum financial revolution is still in its infancy, but its potential impact on the world of finance is undeniable. It is an exciting time to be at the forefront of this revolution, as we continue to unravel the vast possibilities that lie ahead. Stay tuned for the adventurous journey waiting ahead as we explore the uncharted territories of the quantum financial landscape, paving the way for a future where traditional boundaries are transcended, and new frontiers are discovered.

Chapter 6: Securing Financial Systems with Quantum Cryptography

The world of finance has always been under constant threat from malicious actors seeking to exploit vulnerabilities in the system. As technology advances, so do the techniques used by these individuals, making it vital for financial institutions to stay one step ahead in protecting their sensitive data. This is where quantum cryptography comes into play – a revolutionary solution that holds the key to securing financial systems against the looming threat of quantum attacks.

To understand the significance of quantum cryptography, we must first grasp the fundamental principles of quantum mechanics. In the realm of classical computing, information is stored in binary digits, or bits, which represent either a 0 or a 1. In contrast, quantum computing utilizes quantum bits, or qubits, which can exist in a superposition of both 0 and 1 states simultaneously. This unique property of qubits allows for an exponential increase in computational power, posing a significant challenge to traditional encryption methods.

To counter this threat, researchers have turned to another peculiar characteristic of quantum mechanics - the principle of quantum entanglement. This phenomenon refers to the correlation between qubits, where the state of one qubit becomes instantaneously linked to another, regardless of the distance between them. By leveraging quantum entanglement, quantum cryptography offers an unprecedented level of security for transmitting sensitive financial information.

One of the most promising applications of quantum cryptography lies in the field of quantum key distribution (QKD). With QKD, financial institutions can securely exchange encryption keys using the unique properties of quantum physics. Unlike classical encryption methods that rely on computational complexity, QKD uses the fundamental laws of quantum mechanics to detect any unauthorized interception of the transmitted keys. Any attempt to intercept or observe the qubits would inevitably disturb their delicate states, alerting both parties to the presence of an eavesdropper.

Implementing quantum cryptography in financial systems brings numerous benefits. Firstly, it offers a virtually unbreakable security layer that protects against the future onslaught of quantum attacks. As quantum computers become more accessible, the traditional encryption algorithms used in financial transactions could be rendered obsolete overnight. Quantum cryptography provides a robust defense against this looming threat, ensuring the continued privacy and integrity of financial data.

Moreover, quantum cryptography ensures the resilience of financial systems in an increasingly interconnected world. As the global financial network expands, vulnerabilities become more exposed. By integrating QKD into existing infrastructure, financial institutions can safeguard their communications channels, making them impenetrable to even the most advanced attacks.

The future holds great promise for quantum cryptography in revolutionizing the security landscape of financial systems. As researchers continue to advance the field, new quantum-resistant encryption algorithms and techniques are emerging, paving the way for a secure and resilient future. In the second half of this chapter, we will delve deeper into the challenges and potential solutions for integrating quantum cryptography into existing financial systems. Brace yourself for the intriguing journey that lies ahead, as we unlock the power of the quantum financial revolution.Quantum cryptography has the potential to reshape the landscape of financial security, but as with any groundbreaking technology, challenges lie ahead. The successful integration of quantum cryptography into existing financial systems requires careful consideration of various factors, including scalability, cost, and standardization.

One of the primary challenges in implementing quantum cryptography is scalability. Traditional encryption methods are well-established and widely adopted within financial systems, making it difficult to transition to a new and relatively untested technology. Quantum key distribution (QKD) protocols, for instance, often require specialized hardware and infrastructure, limiting their widespread deployment. Significant investments in research and development are necessary to develop scalable quantum cryptographic solutions that can be seamlessly integrated into existing financial networks.

Cost is another crucial factor that needs to be addressed. Quantum cryptography, particularly QKD, tends to be more resource-intensive and expensive compared to classical encryption methods. Financial institutions must carefully weigh the benefits of improved security against the investment required for quantum cryptography implementation. As technologies continue to mature and become more accessible, the cost barrier associated with quantum cryptography is expected to decrease, enabling wider adoption across the financial sector.

Standardization is also vital for the successful implementation of quantum cryptography in financial systems. A standardized framework for quantum cryptographic protocols and algorithms will promote interoperability and ensure the compatibility of different quantum cryptographic implementations. Collaborative efforts between financial institutions, regulatory bodies, and technology firms are necessary to establish industry-wide standards that enable secure communication and cooperation among various entities within the financial sector.

Additionally, the threat landscape surrounding quantum cryptography introduces new challenges. While quantum cryptography addresses the vulnerability of classical encryption methods to quantum attacks, it is not immune to other forms of attacks, such as side-channel attacks or implementation flaws. Ongoing research and rigorous testing are essential to identify and mitigate potential vulnerabilities while ensuring the overall security of quantum cryptographic systems.

Despite these challenges, the potential benefits of quantum cryptography in securing financial systems are undeniable. The integration of quantum-resistant encryption algorithms and techniques will provide a robust defense against the imminent quantum computing threat. Financial institutions that embrace quantum cryptography will be at the forefront of innovation, enjoying unparalleled security and resilience in an increasingly interconnected world.

In conclusion, quantum cryptography offers a transformative solution for enhancing the security and resilience of financial systems. The unique properties of quantum mechanics, such as superposition and entanglement, enable the development of virtually unbreakable encryption methods. However, scalability, cost, standardization, and ongoing research remain critical considerations in successfully integrating quantum cryptography into existing financial systems. As the quantum financial revolution unfolds, it is imperative for financial institutions to embrace the potential of quantum cryptography and collaborate towards a secure and resilient future. The power of quantum cryptography is within reach, and with continued efforts and advancements in the field, the financial sector can confidently navigate the quantum era.

Chapter 7: Quantum-Resistant Encryption for Financial Transactions

In a world where technology rapidly evolves, financial transactions have become a fundamental part of our daily lives. We rely on secure networks to transfer money, make purchases, and manage our finances. However, the rise of quantum computing poses a significant threat to the security of these transactions. As quantum computers gain prominence, the need for quantum-resistant encryption methods becomes crucial in safeguarding sensitive financial data.

Traditional encryption algorithms, such as RSA and ECC (Elliptic Curve Cryptography), have served us well for decades. They rely on hard mathematical problems that would require an impractical amount of time to solve using classical computers. However, these algorithms are vulnerable to attacks from quantum computers. The immense computational power of quantum processors could render these encryption methods obsolete, compromising the confidentiality and integrity of financial transactions.

To tackle this emerging challenge, researchers and cryptographers around the world are actively developing quantum-resistant encryption techniques. These methods aim to provide security against attacks from both classical and quantum computers, ensuring the longevity of financial systems in a post-quantum era.

One promising approach is lattice-based cryptography. Lattice-based encryption schemes leverage the mathematical properties of lattices, which are complex, multi-dimensional mathematical structures. This form of encryption relies on hard problems associated with lattice basis reduction. These problems are believed to be resistant to attacks from quantum computers, making lattice-based cryptography a strong contender for securing financial transactions.

Another notable contender is code-based cryptography. This encryption method relies on error-correcting codes, which introduce redundancy into the message to protect against errors or tampering. The security of code-based cryptography relies on the hardness of decoding specific linear codes, a problem that is known to be difficult even for quantum computers. As a result, code-based encryption offers a potentially robust solution for secure financial transactions in a quantum-powered world.

Furthermore, hash-based signatures have emerged as a reliable and promising approach to quantum-resistant encryption. Unlike traditional digital signatures, hash-based signatures rely on one-way hash functions and merkle trees. These functions are considered mathematically resistant to quantum attacks, providing a secure way to authenticate and verify transactions.

As the race to develop and implement quantum-resistant encryption methods accelerates, financial institutions and regulatory bodies must remain proactive. Collaboration between cryptographers, mathematicians, and financial experts is essential to ensure the successful integration of these new techniques into existing financial systems.

However, challenges persist. The implementation of quantum-resistant encryption methods requires significant computational resources and may introduce new complexities. Additionally, transitioning to these new encryption schemes necessitates careful consideration of interoperability and backward compatibility with existing infrastructure.

The development of quantum computers may still be in its infancy, but it's essential to prepare for their potential impact on the security of financial transactions. By exploring and investing in quantum-resistant encryption methods, we can unlock the power of the future while safeguarding the trust and integrity of our financial systems.

(End of the first half of the chapter)As researchers and cryptographers worldwide work tirelessly to develop quantum-resistant encryption methods, financial institutions and regulatory bodies must remain proactive and open to collaboration. The successful integration of these new techniques into existing financial systems is paramount, requiring the collective efforts of cryptographers, mathematicians, and financial experts.

While there is an urgent need to transition to quantum-resistant encryption methods, various challenges lie ahead. One significant obstacle is the requirement for significant computational resources. Developing and implementing encryption schemes that can withstand quantum attacks demands robust hardware and efficient algorithms capable of performing complex calculations in a timely manner. Financial institutions will need to invest in the necessary computing power to ensure the uninterrupted security of financial transactions.

Another challenge is the potential introduction of new complexities as quantum-resistant encryption methods are integrated into existing infrastructure. Interoperability and backward compatibility with established systems must be carefully considered to minimize disruptions and maximize the seamless adoption of these techniques. Financial institutions should evaluate and plan for potential obstacles that may arise during the implementation process, ensuring a smooth transition and uninterrupted operations.

Furthermore, maintaining a proactive stance against emerging threats is essential. As quantum computing continues to advance, the risk of attacks on conventional encryption methods rises. Financial institutions must regularly reassess their security protocols, keeping pace with the technological advancements of potential adversaries. Continuous monitoring and updating of encryption systems will be crucial in safeguarding sensitive financial data and maintaining customer trust.

In this mission to develop and implement quantum-resistant encryption, financial institutions should also actively engage with regulatory bodies. Collaboration with governmental organizations can help establish standards, guidelines, and regulations that ensure the secure and consistent implementation of quantum-resistant encryption methods across the financial sector. By working together, institutions and regulators can create a robust framework that mitigates the risks posed by quantum computing while fostering innovation and growth within the industry.

As the development of quantum computers continues to progress, it is important to recognize the potential impact they may have on the security of financial transactions. The journey toward quantum-resistant encryption methods is not simply a reactive response to a future threat but a proactive approach to securing our financial systems in an increasingly digital landscape. By exploring and investing in these advanced encryption techniques, we can navigate the path to the future with confidence, ensuring the trust and integrity of our financial systems are preserved.

In conclusion, the rise of quantum computing presents an imminent threat to the security of financial transactions. To address this challenge, researchers and cryptographers are actively developing quantum-resistant encryption methods. Lattice-based cryptography, code-based cryptography, and hash-based signatures are emerging as promising approaches in safeguarding financial data against both classical and quantum attacks. However, the successful integration of these methods will require collaboration, significant computational resources, careful consideration of interoperability, and proactive engagement with regulatory bodies. By embracing these challenges and staying ahead of emerging threats, we can embrace the power of the future while upholding the trust and integrity of our financial systems.

Chapter 8: Challenges and Limitations of Quantum Finance

In the rapidly evolving landscape of finance, where speed and accuracy hold the key to success, quantum computing emerges as a potential game-changer. The immense power and parallel processing capabilities of quantum computers have ignited excitement and curiosity within the financial industry. However, an honest examination of the challenges, limitations, and potential risks associated with the adoption of quantum computing in finance is paramount. Only by understanding and addressing these factors can we fully unlock the potential of the quantum financial revolution.

One significant challenge lies in the development and stability of quantum hardware. Quantum computers are notoriously fragile, requiring carefully controlled environments free from noise and interference to perform optimally. Achieving this level of control is a formidable task, often hindered by the inevitability of environmental disturbances. As a result, building, scaling, and maintaining quantum hardware with the necessary stability and precision pose substantial challenges.

Another key limitation is the scarcity of qualified experts in quantum finance. Harnessing the true power of quantum computing demands a marriage of financial expertise and quantum knowledge. While the financial industry possesses individuals well-versed in traditional finance, the pool of professionals equipped with both financial acumen and quantum expertise remains relatively small. Bridging this knowledge gap requires concerted efforts to educate and train the next generation of quantum-minded financial experts.

Moreover, quantum finance faces significant algorithmic challenges. Traditional financial models and algorithms designed for classical computers may not be optimally suited for quantum systems. While quantum algorithms show immense promise in solving complex problems exponentially faster, adapting and developing algorithms tailored specifically for quantum finance is a complex endeavor. Researchers and practitioners must navigate this uncharted territory to ensure quantum algorithms are both robust and capable of providing reliable results in real-world financial scenarios.

Privacy and security concerns also arise within the realm of quantum finance. Quantum computers possess the ability to break the most commonly used cryptographic protocols, thereby jeopardizing the security of sensitive financial information. While this presents a challenge, it also offers an opportunity to develop quantum-safe encryption methods in anticipation of the quantum era. Collaborative efforts between financial institutions, quantum scientists, and cybersecurity experts become crucial in safeguarding financial systems and data.

Furthermore, regulatory frameworks and ethical considerations must be thoroughly assessed before the widespread adoption of quantum technologies in finance. With great power comes great responsibility, and the potential risks associated with quantum finance require careful evaluation. Ensuring fair and transparent practices, protecting against financial manipulation, and considering the broader societal impact are essential aspects that regulators and industry participants must address in this emerging domain.

As we venture further into the realm of quantum finance, there is no shortage of challenges and limitations to overcome. While the promises of quantum computing and its potential in transforming the financial industry are enticing, a cautious and realistic approach is necessary. The concerted efforts of experts from finance, quantum science, regulatory bodies, and other stakeholders will shape the trajectory of this quantum revolution. Together, we can unlock the full power of the future.

Overcoming the challenges and limitations of quantum finance requires not only technological advancements but also the development of a supportive infrastructure. In the second half of this chapter, we will explore some of the crucial considerations that need to be addressed to unlock the full potential of the quantum financial revolution.

One of the fundamental aspects that require attention is the integration of quantum computing systems with existing financial infrastructure. The transition from classical to quantum systems necessitates careful planning and implementation. Seamless integration requires close collaboration between financial institutions, quantum hardware manufacturers, and software developers. Ensuring compatibility, interoperability, and the optimization of existing financial processes will be essential to capitalize on the power of quantum computing.

Moreover, the scalability of quantum systems poses a significant challenge. While quantum computers have the potential to process and analyze vast amounts of data, the current limitations on the number of qubits severely restrict the size and complexity of problems that can be solved. Developing reliable and scalable quantum hardware will be critical to overcome this limitation.

Another aspect that demands consideration is the verification and validation of quantum financial models. As quantum algorithms are vastly different from classical algorithms, establishing their reliability and accuracy becomes a complex task. Rigorous testing and benchmarking against known financial scenarios, as well as the development of novel validation techniques, will be necessary to ensure the robustness of quantum models and their suitability for real-world applications.

Furthermore, the ethical and social implications of quantum finance must not be overlooked. The potential for algorithms to make high-stakes financial decisions on behalf of individuals or institutions raises questions about accountability and transparency. The impact of these decisions on society at large, as well as potential biases encoded in the algorithms, must be carefully considered. Adopting ethical frameworks and regulatory guidelines are crucial steps to ensure that quantum finance serves the greater good and upholds principles of fairness and equity.

Collaboration and knowledge sharing across disciplines are paramount for the success of quantum finance. Partnerships between academia, industry, and government entities will be essential in driving research, development, and innovation. By fostering interdisciplinary dialogue and cooperation, we can accelerate progress in understanding the intricate interplay between quantum physics and finance, leading to meaningful advancements in this emerging field.

Education and training programs will play a vital role in bridging the quantum knowledge gap within the financial industry. Initiatives that focus on equipping individuals with both financial and quantum expertise will be essential in preparing the future workforce. Universities and professional organizations can play an instrumental role in offering specialized courses and certifications to enable professionals to navigate the quantum financial landscape effectively.

Another key consideration in the future of quantum finance is the need for international collaboration and standardization. Harmonizing regulatory frameworks and ensuring global cooperation is crucial to avoid fragmentation and enable the seamless integration of quantum technologies in the financial sector. International partnerships and agreements can facilitate the exchange of ideas, best practices, and resources to overcome challenges collectively.

In conclusion, the challenges and limitations that quantum finance faces are multidimensional and require careful consideration. From technological hurdles to ethical concerns and societal impacts, resolving these complexities demands collaboration, innovation, and a forward-thinking mindset. By addressing these challenges head-on, we pave the way for a future where the power of quantum computing is harnessed to unlock unprecedented possibilities in the financial industry. The potential benefits are extensive, and with a concerted effort from all stakeholders, we can navigate the path towards a quantum-powered financial revolution.

Chapter 9: Preparing for the Quantum Financial Future

In this rapidly evolving era of technology, where advancements in quantum computing are propelling us towards a new frontier, the financial landscape stands on the brink of a revolutionary transformation. As quantum computers grow increasingly sophisticated, their ability to solve complex problems at an unprecedented speed represents a game-changer for the financial industry. To navigate this uncharted territory, both individuals and financial institutions must proactively prepare for the quantum financial revolution.

For individuals, understanding the potential impact of quantum computing on personal finance is crucial. From investment strategies to day-to-day banking, the quantum era will bring significant changes. Embracing these changes and adapting to the quantum financial future will prove vital for staying ahead of the curve. One key area impacted by quantum computing is cryptography. The cryptographic algorithms that currently secure our financial transactions may become vulnerable to attacks by powerful quantum computers. As such, individuals should be prepared to shift towards quantum-resistant encryption methods to safeguard their financial information.

Moreover, individuals need to recognize the importance of staying informed about upcoming quantum-based financial products. These innovative solutions, designed to leverage the cutting-edge capabilities of quantum computers, have the potential to revolutionize investment opportunities, risk assessment, and portfolio management. Being aware of these emerging options and understanding their underlying principles will provide individuals with a competitive edge in adapting to and harnessing the quantum financial revolution.

Financial institutions, on the other hand, face a more intricate web of challenges and opportunities as they prepare for the quantum financial future. The transition to quantum computing will require a massive shift in infrastructure, expertise, and risk management practices. Traditional banking systems and algorithms will need to be overhauled to accommodate quantum computing's exponential processing power. Designing and implementing quantum-safe cryptographic frameworks will be crucial to ensure the protection of customers' data and financial assets.

Furthermore, financial institutions must cultivate a skilled quantum workforce. Investing in quantum education and training programs will enable professionals to understand and apply the potential of quantum technologies within the financial realm. Hiring quantum experts and collaborating with research institutions will undoubtedly position these institutions at the forefront of the quantum financial revolution.

As we venture further into the quantum era, collaboration and knowledge-sharing among individuals and financial institutions will be key. Establishing multidisciplinary partnerships between quantum scientists, finance experts, and policymakers can accelerate the development of standards, regulations, and ethical guidelines governing quantum finance. This collaborative effort will ensure a smooth and secure transition into the new financial paradigm.

In conclusion... wait, I mean, at the end of this incomplete sentence. The first half of this chapter has provided a glimpse into the quantum financial future and the significance it holds for both individuals and financial institutions. Understanding the potential impact, embracing change, and fostering collaboration will be paramount in successfully navigating the quantum financial revolution. The second half of this chapter will delve deeper into specific strategies for preparing and adapting to the forthcoming quantum era. Stay tuned for the surprising conclusion to our exploration of the quantum financial future.The Quantum Financial Revolution: Unlocking the Power of the Future

Preparing for the Quantum Financial Future (continued)

In this rapidly evolving era of technology, where advancements in quantum computing are propelling us towards a new frontier, the financial landscape stands on the brink of a revolutionary transformation. As quantum computers grow increasingly sophisticated, their ability to solve complex problems at an unprecedented speed represents a game-changer for the financial industry. To navigate this uncharted territory, both individuals and financial institutions must proactively prepare for the quantum financial revolution.

For individuals, the quantum financial future brings about a paradigm shift that demands a proactive approach. Understanding the potential impact of quantum computing on personal finance is crucial. As mentioned earlier, cryptography plays a vital role in ensuring the security of financial transactions. To safeguard their financial information, individuals should familiarize themselves with emerging quantum-resistant encryption methods and be prepared to adopt them when necessary.

Additionally, individuals need to expand their knowledge base to adapt to the changing landscape. As quantum-based financial products begin to emerge, staying informed and understanding their underlying principles will prove invaluable. Quantum computing can revolutionize investment opportunities, risk assessment, and portfolio management. By learning about these innovative solutions and leveraging their potential, individuals can position themselves at the forefront of the quantum financial revolution.

Financial institutions, too, face their own set of challenges and opportunities in preparing for the quantum financial future. The transition to quantum computing necessitates a massive transformation in infrastructure, expertise, and risk management practices. Traditional banking systems and algorithms will require extensive overhauls to accommodate the exponential processing power of quantum computing.

Designing and implementing quantum-safe cryptographic frameworks will be paramount for financial institutions to protect their customers' data and financial assets. Collaborating with quantum experts and research institutions to develop and refine these frameworks ensures that they are best equipped to navigate the evolving threat landscape.

Furthermore, financial institutions must invest in cultivating a skilled quantum workforce. Education and training programs focused on quantum technologies within the financial realm will empower professionals to understand and apply the potential of quantum computing. By having a team of experts well-versed in quantum technologies, financial institutions can effectively explore and exploit the opportunities that emerge in the quantum financial future.

As we venture further into the quantum era, collaboration and knowledge-sharing among individuals and financial institutions become indispensable. Establishing multidisciplinary partnerships between quantum scientists, finance experts, and policymakers can accelerate the development of standards, regulations, and ethical guidelines governing quantum finance. By working together, we can ensure a smooth and secure transition into this new financial paradigm.

In conclusion, the first half of this chapter has provided a glimpse into the quantum financial future and the significance it holds for both individuals and financial institutions. Understanding the potential impact, embracing change, and fostering collaboration will be paramount in successfully navigating the quantum financial revolution.

Now armed with a foundation of knowledge, individuals and financial institutions can begin to explore specific strategies for preparing and adapting to the forthcoming quantum era. The second half of this chapter will delve deeper into these strategies, outlining practical steps and insights that will assist in harnessing the power of the quantum financial revolution.

Stay tuned for the surprising conclusion to our exploration of the quantum financial future.

Chapter 10: The Societal Impact of Quantum Finance

In recent years, the integration of quantum computing and finance has sparked significant interest and anticipation. The potential implications of this convergence extend far beyond the realm of finance, reaching into various aspects of our society. As quantum computing continues to develop, it has the power to revolutionize the way we approach financial systems, decision-making processes, and even socioeconomic structures.

One of the most significant societal impacts resulting from the integration of quantum computing and finance lies in the realm of data analysis. Traditional financial systems rely heavily on statistical models and historical data to make predictions and inform decision-making. However, quantum computing has the potential to enhance this process by analyzing vast amounts of data at an unprecedented speed, enabling more accurate predictions and risk assessments.

With quantum computing's ability to process and interpret complex financial data sets, financial institutions will be better equipped to detect anomalies and anticipate market trends. This could potentially lead to more efficient risk management strategies and enhanced stability within the financial sector. Moreover, the ability to analyze data in real-time may enable the identification of complex patterns and correlations that were previously undetectable, allowing for more informed investment decisions.

The integration of quantum computing and finance also has the potential to reshape the notion of security and privacy. Quantum cryptography, for instance, offers an unparalleled level of cryptographic security by harnessing the principles of quantum physics. As financial transactions increasingly occur in a digital landscape, the adoption of quantum encryption methods can safeguard sensitive information from malicious attacks, thus bolstering trust in online financial systems.

Furthermore, quantum computing may pave the way for the development of more sophisticated algorithms that can tackle socioeconomic challenges. For example, optimization algorithms powered by quantum computing can address complex problems such as resource allocation and distribution, urban planning, or even climate change mitigation. By considering multiple variables and constraints simultaneously, these algorithms may offer innovative and sustainable solutions to societal problems.

It is crucial to note that the full potential of quantum finance extends beyond the limits of our current understanding. As quantum computing continues to advance, so too will our comprehension of its capabilities and implications. However, we must also acknowledge the potential risks that come hand in hand with this revolutionary technology.

In the second half of this chapter, we will delve deeper into the challenges and ethical considerations associated with quantum finance. From the ethical implications of data privacy in a quantum-powered financial landscape to the potential for increased socioeconomic disparity, we will explore the multifaceted nature of this groundbreaking integration. Stay tuned as we navigate through the uncharted territories of the quantum financial revolution...

... end of the sentence.In the second half of this chapter, we will further explore the challenges and ethical considerations associated with the integration of quantum computing and finance. As with any revolutionary technology, there are risks and concerns that must be addressed to ensure the responsible and equitable use of this powerful tool.

One significant ethical consideration in quantum finance revolves around data privacy. With the ability of quantum computing to process vast amounts of data at unprecedented speeds, there arises a need for robust regulations and safeguards to protect individuals' personal information. As financial systems become increasingly reliant on quantum-powered technologies, it is crucial to establish a comprehensive framework that ensures the privacy and security of individuals' data. Striking the right balance between innovation and data protection will be paramount in maintaining public trust in these systems.

Another ethical concern lies in the potential for an increased socioeconomic disparity resulting from the adoption of quantum finance. While this technology holds promise in addressing complex socioeconomic challenges, there is a risk that it could exacerbate existing inequalities if not managed thoughtfully. Access to quantum-powered financial systems and advanced algorithms should be made available to all, regardless of socioeconomic status. This requires proactive measures to bridge the digital divide, provide equal opportunities for education and training, and ensure inclusive participation in the benefits offered by quantum finance.

Furthermore, the reliance on quantum computing and algorithms in financial decision-making raises questions about accountability and transparency. As financial institutions increasingly rely on complex algorithms driven by quantum computing, it becomes essential to have clear guidelines and regulations in place to ensure fairness, prevent discrimination, and guard against the potential for unintended biases. Understandable and transparent models must be developed to ensure that individuals affected by the decisions made by these algorithms can comprehend and trust the outputs.

The integration of quantum computing and finance also brings forth concerns regarding system vulnerabilities. While quantum cryptography offers a higher level of security, it is not immune to potential attacks. Malicious actors may exploit vulnerabilities in quantum-powered financial systems, posing risks to data integrity and financial stability. It is imperative for researchers and industry practitioners to collaborate in the development of robust security measures that can adapt to emerging threats effectively.

Lastly, the rapid advancement of quantum computing in finance necessitates continual assessment of its impact on employment and workforce dynamics. While this technology has the potential to increase efficiency and streamline processes, it may also lead to shifts in job requirements and workforce displacement. Ensuring a just transition for those affected by these changes will require investment in retraining and upskilling programs to equip individuals with the knowledge and skills needed for the evolving job market.

As we conclude this chapter on the societal impact of quantum finance, it is vital to recognize that the integration of quantum computing and finance presents both immense potential and complex challenges. By addressing these challenges through thoughtful regulation, promoting inclusivity, transparency, and proactive risk management, we can navigate the uncharted territories of the quantum financial revolution responsibly. The fusion of quantum computing with finance offers transformative possibilities for our society, but it is our collective responsibility to ensure that its benefits are distributed equitably and its risks mitigated effectively.

Together, we must embrace this journey with curiosity, caution, and a steadfast commitment to creating a future in which the power of quantum finance is harnessed for the greater good of humanity.

The End